About the Author

Originally from Antwerp, Belgium, Hugh Van Es moved to Bangkok, Thailand, in July of 1987 with his parents. During more than three decades of living and working in Thailand, he has been employed in various international conglomerates, such as Swarovski, while he just founded his own company Proquanet in December 2022.

Hell in Paradise

Hugh Van Es

Hell in Paradise

Olympia Publishers
London

www.olympiapublishers.com
OLYMPIA PAPERBACK EDITION

Copyright © Hugh Van Es 2023

The right of Hugh Van Es to be identified as author of
this work has been asserted in accordance with sections 77 and 78 of
the Copyright, Designs and Patents Act 1988.

All Rights Reserved

No reproduction, copy or transmission of this publication
may be made without written permission.
No paragraph of this publication may be reproduced,
copied or transmitted save with the written permission of the publisher,
or in accordance with the provisions
of the Copyright Act 1956 (as amended).

Any person who commits any unauthorized act in relation to
this publication may be liable to criminal
prosecution and civil claims for damage.

A CIP catalogue record for this title is
available from the British Library.

ISBN: 978-1-80439-080-1

This is a work of creative nonfiction.
The events are portrayed to be the best of the author's memory. While
all the stories in this book are true, some names and identifying details
have been changed to protect the privacy of the people involved.

First Published in 2023

Olympia Publishers
Tallis House
2 Tallis Street
London
EC4Y 0AB

Printed in Great Britain

Dedication

I dedicate this book to two of the strongest women in my life. First to my mother, who inspired me to start reading at a young age, and secondly to my wife, who insisted I go search for my friends, thereby igniting the spark which resulted in this story being written.

Acknowledgments

Thank you to all the characters in the story, who gave me such positive reviews, which provided me with the courage to actually get the book published.

One man's quest to search for his friends after the 2004 tsunami in the South of Thailand.

(Based on true events)

Prologue

For about a year and half, I'd been working for a company which was based in the Middle East. A company established well over a hundred years ago, manufacturing high-quality products for the luxury market. An organization built on age-old traditions and with a long history, but also a company where there was no room for advancement. Where I had been passed over for promotion not once, not twice, but three times, just because I was not able to speak Arabic. A company where I worked very late hours without overtime compensation and where for every minute I arrived late, my salary was deducted. An organization where the owner ruled by fear and everything was micro-managed.

On one occasion, during one of the frequent visits by the owner, he used to sit down with the management for lunch every day. One day, the table was set up wrongly by the maid, who had switched the fork and knife at the place of the boss at the head of the table. "Who did this?" he remarked angrily. "Who does not know how to set a table? Tell me, right now!"

The GM at that time, Kevin, stammered, "Ah, sir, the maid Auntie Som arranged the table, our apologies."

"Where is she, bring her here now!" he shouted, turning red in the face. When poor old Auntie Som, who had turned 59 years old just the day before, got to the table, she was clearly scared out of her wits and shocked when the owner fired her on the spot right there and then. With tears in her eyes, she walked away dejectedly, shocked that her fifteen years of service with the company had been terminated so brutally for such a small reason.

Two days later, during the final meeting with the management, all relevant stakeholders were present. Everyone was there, packed in the room, forcing some people to stand during the many hours of discussions. You could feel the tension in the room with nervous beads of sweat slowly dripping off some of the faces.

After lots of back and forth to discuss the product samples, he was clearly dissatisfied with something because he started berating the head of production in Arabic in front of everyone. While I did not understand a word he said, it was clear that the poor guy was being bitched at like there was no tomorrow. So, the meeting ended with an unhealthy dose of stress and pressure for all concerned while the owner went on his merry way, back to the airport for a trip back home on his own private jet. Ah, the perks of being a multi-millionaire. When my son Damian was born a few weeks later, the company deducted three days' worth of salary because I wanted to be there for the birth. It was, therefore, completely natural that I started looking for a new job. I mean why spend so much of my time for so little reward and so much stress. I swore to myself that if I ever made it to the top executive position of a company, I would know exactly how NOT to manage a business.

You could then also understand why I jumped at the chance when my brother Bob called to ask me if I was still looking for work. "Well duh," I told him. He explained that the position was that of operations manager at a Belgian company. A company well advanced in the manufacturing of ideal cut diamonds. Once again, an enterprise with a long history behind it in terms of name and fame. "Hell yes," I exclaimed. I arranged for the interview for the following Tuesday. Let's see if I could go present myself to show them that I would make the best candidate to fill their needs!

Chapter 1

Tuesday 14 March 2004, I arrived at my interview at one forty-five p.m., fifteen minutes before the appointment. My mom always said that it was better to be half an hour early than five minutes late. It was a long, two story factory building painted orange. That's interesting, I remarked. Didn't see many orange-colored factories out there. I was received by the receptionist and taken to a large meeting room. I was offered a coffee and some water. Within a few minutes, the Managing Director, Erwin, stormed into the room, full of bustle and energy and with a million-dollar smile. I learned later on that he had a teeth-bleaching a few weeks prior to the interview, and my God did his teeth sparkle. I wondered if those pearly whites would glow under a black light. He shook my hand vigorously. Fully shaven, he was slightly shorter than I was but looked well over 100kgs. His infectious smile and jovial manner immediately put me at ease and my nervousness dissipated a bit.

I must say Erwin was making quite an impression. Here was a guy who started polishing diamonds at the young age of twelve. Together with Jean Paul, the owner of the company, they learned all stages of diamond processing from the experts in Antwerp. He had come to Thailand four years prior to set up the factory on behalf of the owner, his childhood friend. While he had managed the company those first few years, they were now searching for an operations manager, a position well suited to my experience, to further expand the business.

The interview took well over four hours, clearly showing that this was a job with prospects, a job at a company that was about to expand, and a company with a clear future. Erwin took me on a very detailed tour of the factory which was very impressive. I could already show off my Thai linguistic abilities by addressing some of the staff directly during the tour. Nice to see a few smiles from Erwin, who after four years in Thailand already spoke a very impressive level of Thai himself. It was also cool to learn that I had a lot of things in common with Erwin, the MD, making me excited that this was going to be an amazing opportunity. When I finally got home, Lek had been worried sick. "Where have you been these last four hours?" she questioned.

"At the interview," I said. "It went fantastic! They loved me!"

I was therefore ecstatic and very excited to learn a few weeks later, after two more interviews, one of which was during a dinner at an Italian restaurant, that I had landed the job. I could hardly contain my smile when I tendered my resignation to the latest Arabic-speaking GM, giving them my two months' notice. You could understand that these two months were the longest of my life. I did the bare minimum all the while reading up on the new company and preparing myself for the new job.

I joined the new company on the 1st of June 2004. The reception on that first day was incredible. After working in Thailand for all these years, I was finally being treated like a true expat. Erwin himself picked me up at reception. He personally brought me to my own private office, right next to his on the second floor. I had my own office, oh my God, with a large window looking into the factory. At the previous company, I shared a tiny office with three other persons with no views of the outside world. What a huge difference. I sat down and noticed a stack of business cards, already prepared with my name, Hugh Van Es, and position, Operations Manager. A small fridge stood in the corner. Erwin himself walked over and opened it: "We don't know what you like yet, so we have filled it with Coke, Fanta, Sprite, some water and a few sodas. If you like something else, just let us know." I tried not to look too shocked but was very pleased to say the least.

The first few months absolutely flew by. Erwin and I grew together professionally and worked closely together day in and day out, enlarging the factory and doubling its workforce within a few short months. We set up systems and new processes, and standardized many areas. It was great to brainstorm together and discuss everything openly. I felt like a true part of the management team, and we decided everything together.

On a personal level, it was clear we were also growing closer. The first dinner with the wives was scheduled within the first month. If we were going to be working closely, we needed to meet the wives. One of the company drivers picked us up from home and took us to La Paola Italian restaurant at the end of Sukhumvit Soi 13. Just a little hole in the wall, with very low ceilings and only three to four tables furnished as a rustic Italian kitchen, with checkered tablecloths, dated paintings of everything Italian, landscapes, ruins, and of course Italian foods. Erwin and Sabrina were already there, having just gotten there themselves. We made the round of introductions, immediately going for the three kiss Belgian greeting. Erwin, with his outgoing personality started boasting. "Here, at La Paolo, you don't have to order. We eat whatever Mama cooks," he stated while pointing at an old Italian lady sitting in the corner drinking a glass of red wine. "It cannot get more authentic than this, believe me." He turned to the Italian manager Paolo, who was

Mama's son and said, "Paolo, we are hungry, just give us the full menu. As for drinks, I'll have a gin and tonic, the ladies will each have a glass of white wine, and Hugh will have a Chivas Coke."

That first talk was heartwarming, touching subject after subject. One Italian dish after another kept arriving. A platter of cold cuts, mixed vegetables, a basket of breads, and bruschetta with tomatoes. All different pastas, spaghetti, linguini, ravioli, as well as antipasti, it kept coming. It was clear, Erwin could drink. I tried to keep up and matched him glass for glass. Soon however it was clear, he was getting ahead. While my glass was still two-thirds full, his was already getting close to empty. We talked, we laughed, we got seriously drunk.

Then the desserts, it just kept coming. Tiramisu, Pannacotta, assorted chocolates and cakes, you name it, it was there. I had never in my life eaten such an extensive variety of different Italian foods. It was turning into a fantastic evening. The wives got along, Erwin and I were getting along. It was just a fantastic feeling. After the two years of absolutely horrible stress and pressure in the previous job, I was now in a job that I loved, that had a future, and it required working for absolutely kind and wonderful people. It couldn't get any better than this. Oh, but it did.

By about eleven p.m., the last couple left the restaurant and we now had the place to ourselves. Erwin suddenly got up and told us he loved this song and took Sabrina by the hand, pulled her up out of her chair and started dancing with her. "Join us, Lek and Hugh," he said, so Lek and I got out of our chairs, a bit wobbly from all the drinks and joined them in slow dancing to the music. After a few minutes, Erwin said, "Changez", and grabbed Lek while I continued dancing with Sabrina. Erwin, ever the charmer, twirled Lek around, showing off his dancing skills.

The song ended and we all sat back down.

While Lek and I were both stuffed to the gills, and were seriously inebriated, Paolo came with a platter, four small shot glasses and two carafes. "Would anyone care for a little Coffee-cello or Limon-cello?" he crooned in his Italian accent.

"Oh, you have to try this," Erwin bellowed. "This is so smooth, it's a digestive."

I looked at Lek, who was clearly not in the mood for such a shot, and while my mind was shouting NOOOOOO, I turned to Erwin and said, "Sure, we'll try the Limoncello." After so much food and drink, I tell you, this did NOT hit the spot. It burned all the way down, trying not to make a face of disgust, I told Erwin, "Hmmm, yummy." I urgently took a sip of my Chivas Coke to take the taste away.

We said our goodbyes, have a nice weekend, and we stumbled to the car. Lek and I fell in, seriously drunk, and the driver set off. After we made two turns, in the back alleys of Sukhumvit, we both shouted at the same time, "Stop the car" and we hung out the window and puked out our dinner. Safe to say, we managed to get home and fell in bed without a shower, woke the next morning with the mother of all hangovers. What an introductory evening, my lord.

Chapter 2

Sooner, rather than later, they invited us over to their house. This time, a delicious meal of traditional Belgian fare was prepared by Sabrina. We drank, ate, laughed and joked, and enjoyed a wonderful evening. It was clear we were becoming close friends.

Of course, we returned the favor and invited them both to our house. The kids were still awake and enjoyed the funny antics from Erwin, making them giggle. After a while, we started playing some games. "Do you have any coins?" he asked. Lek brought him a handful of coins which he stacked on the corner of his elbow. He flicked his arm down and managed to catch all the coins in his hand. Wow, what a cool trick. Erwin, while sitting on the floor, then jokingly started to stick all the coins on his face. Amazingly, he managed to keep them all sticking for quite some time, earning delighted laughter from the kids. Later that evening, I learned from Lek that Thai people believed it was bad luck to stick coins on one's face. As I fell asleep, I briefly thought if this was an omen but soon passed it off as just another Thai superstition.

Merry Christmas, everyone! Saturday, December 25, 2004, we were packing our suitcases for a well-deserved holiday in Koh Chang, a holiday destination about four hours' drive east of Bangkok, very close to the Cambodian border. I had been living here for over seventeen years and had never visited this island, the second largest one in Thailand after Phuket in the South.

Erwin and his wife Sabrina were looking forward to the scuba diving trip at the Similan Islands in the South of Thailand. They were avid divers and had traveled the world to do so. Easy, of course, when you didn't have children.

Erwin and Sabrina flew directly to Phuket on Saturday, for further transportation to the islands. Lek and I rose at four a.m., woke the kids, got them dressed and fed and we were ready to set out by five thirty a.m. on Sunday the 26th of December. This was to be our first major holiday since the birth of our youngest, Damian, who at the age of two, was still very much a baby with all the extra effort that brought.

After about half an hour's drive, cruising along the Bangkok-Chonburi Motorway, listening to some 70s hits, Tasha, our oldest at about five years of age said: "Papi, Papi, my tummy hurts! I need to go to the toilet!" Oh, wasn't that lovely, I thought. We had just left home and we already had a pooper!

"Hold it for a moment, love, let me find a gas station with a bathroom," I said. Our oldest seemed to have eaten something wrong the day before and it was turning into an unpleasant drive, what with a two-year-old boy, that still needed diaper changes and milk bottles, and a five-year-old girl, who had a bad case of the shits. We hoped that it wasn't a sign that would influence the holiday. We finally found a decent gas station with proper bathrooms and took care of business.

About a good two hours into the drive to the east, I suddenly realized that I forgot, for the first time in my life, my mobile phone. I immediately felt like shit. How could I forget my fucking phone on a holiday which included a long road trip? Right away, Lek started going through her handbag (one of those big bulky ones that fitted everything, and it took you forever to find something) and thank God Almighty that she had brought hers, one of those early Sony Ericsson models. Damn, one second later, we realized that there were only three blocks of battery life left on her phone (out of five) and no charger. No problem, we said, being the optimists that we were, we would just go buy it over there, and so continued in good spirits onwards. I must admit that a little doubt was now starting to creep into the back of my mind. First Tasha's shits and now this? Focus on the positives, Hugh, I told myself. We were going on holiday! I brought my mind back to the drive at hand, which was actually turning into a wonderful journey eastwards, with the sun rising, clear blue skies and some good tunes to listen to. On the way, we passed Rayong, Chanthaburi, Klaeng and finally reached the turn off to Koh Chang.

Once we arrived at the pier, to take the ferry across, we had some spare time. So, what did Thai people do when they had time to kill? They ate. We sat down in a small noodle shop next to the pier and ordered a round of noodles. Lek of course took hers with loads of chilis, turning it into a red soup. I took mine without any spices, mainly because I didn't like spicy foods, even after almost two decades here. To me, spices took the taste away from the food. I mean, how could you properly sample the food when your mouth was on fire and you were sweating like a pig? Surely your taste buds were burnt to a crisp! And let's not even consider the morning after eating spicy food, because you could enjoy the burn all over again, but at the other side. A 17" TV, hanging from a rickety pole in the corner, was set to the local news, where we heard, for the first time, about the massive earthquake in Banda Aceh in Indonesia.

"Damn, 9.1 on the Richter Scale!" I exclaimed. "That was horrible. Wasn't that the largest ever in recent times?" I asked Lek who wasn't sure. At that time, it was about ten a.m., so the deadly wave was still on its way to the south of Thailand. Little did we know!

Tasha, in her innocence, asked me, "Papi, what's an earthquake?"

"Well, sweetie, it's when the ground shakes back and forth," I said while I grabbed her under the arms and shook her vigorously from left to right, generating quite a lot of giggles.

Obviously, Damian right away chimed in, "Me too, Papi, me too." Sure enough, when I did the same to him, I received another round of warm, heart-melting baby laughter, which made us all laugh out loud, to the merriment of the shop owners. All the while we were enjoying the last of our noodle soup, and getting ready to drive on to the ferry, we and many thousands of Thai people were clueless that a colossal tsunami was on its way which would cause billions of dollars' worth of damages, would kill over two hundred thousand people globally and affect the lives of millions of people around the world.

Chapter 3

We did not give it another thought, as our minds were firmly fixed on getting on the ferry, arriving to the hotel, and getting the kids to the pool so that we could start relaxing. After parking our car on the ferry, we took a long steep staircase to the top where we had uninterrupted views of the ocean and the island in the distance. The kids absolutely loved it and were chattering and running around like two little monkeys. The ferry ride took us about forty-five minutes. The drive from the ferry to the hotel was absolutely gorgeous. One single two-lane road went around most of the island, although it did not complete the loop. Twisting and turning, up and down we soaked it all in. Lush, thick vegetation on one side, and crystal blue waters on the other. As the temperature was a cool twenty-six degrees, we turned off the car's aircon and opened all the windows. Boney M's "Ma Baker" was playing on the radio. After a thirty-minute drive, we finally reached the Sea View Resort & Spa. We checked in at the hotel and while signing all the documents we drank our welcome drink of watered-down punch. When we reached the room, we were nicely surprised to find a very spacious suite arranged with two extra beds for the children.

Both Tasha and Damian were dressed and ready in their suits before we even finished unpacking our bags. So Lek and I threw on our bathing suits, lathered ourselves and the kids up with sun cream and set out to explore the hotel.

The hotel was amazing. Large grounds with beautiful

gardens with all the amenities you needed: two swimming pools, one right on the beach, canoes, snorkeling equipment, a ping-pong table and the beach itself was absolutely stunning. Fine white sand with lots of trees with a small island a few hundred meters out in the sea. We swam all day and played with the kids in the sand, and even built a sand castle. When we got back to our room, we ordered room service, and gave the kids a shower. The kid's Thai blood ensured that both were already nicely tanned, even after only half a day at the pool. It was around six p.m. so it was already getting dark outside. The kids fell asleep before their food arrived, and while Lek and I were enjoying our dinner, me a club sandwich, while Lek took a fried basil leaf with squid, we finally saw the extent of the damage the earthquake caused on TV. It had resulted in a massive tsunami that had caused havoc, destruction and death in many countries, all the way to Africa. To our astonishment and dismay, we saw how Thailand's southern region had been devastated. The whole afternoon, while we were enjoying our vacation, we were oblivious to what had happened earlier that day. By leaving my phone at home, I had no idea if anyone had tried to call me.

This was a disaster of horrific proportions. It was then that I decided to call Jean Paul, the owner of the company, to align myself with him. He informed me that repeated phone calls to Erwin were not being answered so worry was really starting to creep in. I told Jean Paul that I would spend as much time as possible listening to the local news and if I heard anything, I would give him a call. "Night and day, anytime, Hugh, call me when you hear something," Jean Paul insisted. I spent most of that first night glued to the Thai TV news, which was broadcasting live, trying to pick up any word on the Similan Islands but heard nothing, stressing me out to no end. I fell into a restless sleep around four a.m.

Full of worry, the next day, Monday, after a quick breakfast we decided to drive out to look for a new phone charger for Lek, as we had almost run out of battery. It was pure hell, knowing that in this situation when it was of the utmost importance to have a working phone, it took us forever to find a shop on the island that had the correct model. We finally found one in the fourth shop we came to.

Then, back at the hotel, while the kids were playing in the sand, under the watchful eye of Lek, I was on the phone all day with Jean Paul, who was on his way from Beijing with his family, to spend New Year's Eve in Bangkok. I was also in constant contact with Sommai, the General Manager of the factory, to see if he could help from Bangkok to determine where they were staying. Sommai was lucky, finding information at the factory that showed that Erwin had booked his hotel through the company.

With dread and a very heavy heart, we found out that Erwin had booked his room at the Sofitel Hotel in Kao Lak, the worst hit area in Thailand. Repeated SMS and phone calls to both Erwin and Sabrina were still met with a ringing phone. We were trying to stay positive, thinking that as long as the phone was ringing, things were okay. Knowing the type of people that they were, they were surely helping out others who were worse off, without worrying about themselves. I agreed with Jean Paul that I would cut my holiday short, drive down to Bangkok the next day and come to Phuket to go look for both of them.

Tuesday morning, 28th of December, we checked out from the hotel at six a.m., skipped breakfast, to the consternation of the kids, and drove as fast as humanly possible to Bangkok, while keeping in mind that I was driving on Thailand's deadly roads.

We stopped along the way to get some snacks and drinks for the long drive back. Upon arrival in Bangkok, I dropped Lek and the kids at home, threw some clothes in an overnight bag and drove to Don Muang International airport reaching there around four p.m. I bought the first available ticket to Phuket, and after going through security, I waited at a full domestic airport for the next plane to Phuket. While I sat for up to three hours at the gate waiting to board my plane, it was clear that most of the tourists, waiting for their flights, were those who had changed their holiday plans at the last minute and were on the way to Koh Samui in the gulf, which was not affected by the tsunami.

These three hours I spent sitting there waiting for my plane to the disaster zone were horrible in that the televisions at the gate were all showing the gruesome images of the tsunami over and over again. Indonesia, Thailand, India, the list went on and on of countries that were devastated by the earthquake's tsunami. One small consolation while viewing these images from afar was that I was sitting far enough not to hear the commentary.

While driving down from Koh Chang earlier that morning, Khun Pot, Erwin's driver, had called me and asked me if he could take the company car, get a buddy, and drive down to Kao Lak to help look for Erwin, as he could not just sit around idly in Bangkok and be sick with worry. Pot had been their driver for almost the full four years in Thailand, so he knew them through and through. I agreed to it right away and told him I would meet them there tonight. "Please drive safe," I told him.

Jean Paul had landed in Bangkok from Beijing earlier in the day and was able to get a connecting flight for early afternoon so he was first to arrive in Phuket. Upon exiting the plane, carrying his overnight bag, he walked to the taxi counter and booked a ride directly to the Sofitel in Kao Lak. On the way there, the taxi driver asked him in broken English if he wanted to visit any temples. Jean Paul politely declined not realizing, at that moment, that most of the bodies were by then being taken to the local temples but asked him to stop at every hospital they passed on the way there. Asking the taxi to wait, Jean Paul jumped into each hospital they drove by to no avail. No signs from Erwin or Sabrina. By then it was well into the evening and darkness had come. Suddenly, Jean Paul realized, when they were about to reach the hotel, that he was actually following a pickup truck piled with bodies. His heart sank. When he arrived, completely stressed out, at the hotel, he got out of the taxi on shaky legs, still picturing the horrific scene of a few moments earlier. By a stroke of luck, he met Pot and his friend from the factory, Songkran, who had just arrived by car at the hotel themselves. They tried to enter the hotel, only to be turned away by the security guards who had little or no information. Dejected, they got in the car together and drove back to Phuket, anxious that they still had not reached Erwin or Sabrina.

Chapter 4

I landed at eight p.m. in Phuket, where I immediately hired a taxi to take me to the nearest hospital, where I started looking at all the announcement boards, full of photos of missing people. Against the wishes of the nurses, I walked and talked my way into many hospital wards to find the couple but to no avail. I guess being fluent in Thai helped, because as a foreigner, most were usually shocked that a 'farang' could speak Thai, so it helped to open a few doors. I even gathered up the courage and entered the morgue, which was nice and cool, compared to the outside temperature. Only a few of the overhead lights were working, casting a weird gloom over the room. The smell of disinfectant was strong, and it clung to the back of my throat. Luckily (or so I thought at the time) they were not there. During that first drive around town, it seemed Phuket was left mostly unscathed. Little did I know that the scene on the other side of the island was vastly different. There, the monster wave DID hit the island.

It took Jean Paul, Pot and Songkran a very long time to get back from Kao Lak, so I entered the nearest copy shop to make copies of their photos, so that I could stick them on all the message boards which we were sure to pass the next day. The taxi then took me to one of the hotels where I booked rooms for the four of us. Later that night, I met up with the three of them and we decided to go to the district office in Phuket town to find the Belgian Embassy Representative. I didn't recall his name, but he looked to be just a visa man who didn't know anything, which added to our frustrations.

After many hours of hardly eating, we arrived back at the hotel after midnight, starving. The staff were nice enough to wake the cook who rounded us up some fried rice. We got to bed around two or three a.m. and hardly slept a wink before waking very early the next morning to drive down to Kao Lak. We stopped at the local hospital to get some gloves, disinfectant, and mouth masks. We also stopped at a 7-Eleven for some iced coffees and snacks. The drive took us over two hours through magnificently beautiful scenery, full of rolling hills covered with lush green vegetation. Once we turned off the main road, we drove up a very curving road through the hills, twisting and turning, and finally drove down and arrived at the seaside.

When we reached Kao Lak, the scene that greeted us, was one of total desolation and destruction. It was now Wednesday morning, the 29th of December 2004, around eight a.m., three days after the catastrophe. Everywhere you looked you saw carnage. Overturned cars, smashed houses, sand everywhere, even vans on top of houses, completely bashed in. Uprooted trees and broken-down electricity poles, with their wires all tangled up. The road was completely covered with sand and debris. We even spotted a large fishing vessel upside down against the side of a house. It was a wretched sight. The worst thing was, that right behind this picture of total ruin, was the ocean, crystal-clear aquamarine-blue water against a vivid blue sky with the sun beating down on us, at a comfortable twenty-six degrees centigrade. I had never seen the sea so tranquil, serene and clean. It was hell in a picturesque setting. We drove slowly through the town, in total silence, in awe of what mother nature had unleashed.

We drove onwards seemingly for the longest time till we finally reached the Sofitel Hotel. Upon arrival, our hearts sank deep into our stomachs as our eyes beheld once again complete destruction. The main building structure of the hotel, which was a U-shaped building constructed around a large pool in the center, was still standing, but the rest was a nightmare. Sand, tree branches, beach chairs, canoes, umbrellas, all tumbled up and scattered across the lobby and against the side of the building. When we located someone in charge, we started asking questions. We knew that they had gone scuba diving early Sunday morning, so we wanted to know from the hotel where they had gone. The manager, a French guy, told us that the hotel itself did not have a scuba diving service, but that they outsourced it to a local shop a bit further up around Takua Pa town. When we were about to leave to follow this new lead, some commotion happened as a rescue staff brought a stack of passports. We waited to see if Erwin and Sabrina's were included, and they were. Okay, that was at least something. We had their passports, but not them, which didn't mean anything yet. They went scuba diving after all, and since the hotel did not have this service, we would find them soon, as we now had a concrete lead to follow, which got our hopes up. Unfortunately, the hotel could not hand the passports over to us, but would do so to the Belgian Embassy Representative, set up in Phuket District Office, in the center of Phuket.

We then set out on our way to find this shop. On the way we passed some hospitals, so decided to stop there and check if they were there, and to hang up some posters. Looking at the hospital's announcement boards as well as a quick peek into the wards did not provide any further leads, so we continued on our way. We finally arrived at Takua Pa town where, after some searching and asking around for directions, we located the Director of Activities of the Sofitel Hotel. It was obvious my Thai language was coming in handy, as most of them did not speak any English. From these people, who remembered both Erwin and Sabrina, we learned that yes, they had come to the shop that morning, but strangely, the boat's engine was broken that day and they could not have sailed out to the islands. After all day trying to follow the lead and trying to puzzle together what they had done, still in high hopes that we would be finding them any time now, we were finally faced with the news that we did not want to hear. They had come here, to find a defective boat, so the only thing that they could have done was to go back to the hotel. Damn, this was not what we wanted to hear. Sick with worry, we got back in the car. While I was talking to the activities director, Khun Pot had heard from someone around there, that most bodies found in the Sofitel Hotel, were being transported to the Takua Pa Temple, so we decided to drive there.

Now you had to realize, that everywhere we went, we had to drive about five kilometers per hour, as the roads were strewn with debris, and everywhere you had cars driving around with the same purpose as us, to find their loved ones. We continued to zig zag ourselves around all the obstacles in the road. Another added predicament was that our mobiles seemed to work very poorly. Every phone call was met with a NETWORK BUSY signal, or just busy. You had to try at least ten to fifteen times before you could get through to any number, and then many times, with a bad quality connection, which, if it fell out, would start the whole dialing up process again.

Chapter 5

It was about three thirty p.m., when we finally arrived at the temple, which was packed with people. Before we found a parking spot, we already noticed hundreds of bodies, shrouded in thin, white sheets lying in neat rows in the distance.

We stepped out of the car, and then, like a Mike Tyson uppercut, the smell hit us. It was just awful. You could not describe it, nor could you compare it to any of our known bad smells. Rotten eggs, a baby's diaper and even that stink-bomb you used to play with as a kid, did not even come close. It was absolutely nauseating. Thank God we hadn't eaten anything all day, otherwise we would have surely been vomiting on the spot. We took the stuff from the hospital out of the booth of the car. We put on two pairs of surgical gloves, sprayed our shoes with disinfectant, and put on three mouth masks on top of each other, each one, soaked in the liquid form of VapoRub. We had put on so much, that our eyes were watering. Tears streamed down our cheeks, wetting the mouth masks, and still we could smell it. It penetrated everything and got stuck in the back of our throats. Slowly, with beating hearts and shaky legs, and with nervous sweat breaking out, we headed into the temple.

The closer we came, the worse it got. The hundreds of bodies we thought it was, were actually stretching out further in the back, adding to the gruesome scene. There must have been close to five hundred bodies here. The row of corpses continued into a wooden sala of the temple, making it even darker in there. We stumbled like zombies through the first rows, thinking how to start this task. Most bodies were tightly wrapped with an off-white-colored shroud, tied in three different places, around the feet, the waist and the upper body. How the hell were we going to find them like this? I thought. Did we really have to untie those knots, and open the cloth? Here and there, some shrouds had loosened, and the sight was one of pure horror, straight out of a Stephen King novel. Black, bloated faces, tongues sticking out of engorged lips, arms and legs twisted in unnatural angles, swollen to outrageous proportions, I was in hell. With a heartbeat of a hundred and forty, I continued through the rows, just trying to look for Erwin and Sabrina. I could not bring myself to open the shrouds yet, so I just staggered on, trying to understand the enormous task ahead of us.

After wandering through row after row of cadavers for twenty minutes, all of a sudden, Pot called out, calling us over. When we got there, he told me in Thai, he thought he had found Erwin. Here we stood in front of a blackened, engorged corpse with the shroud pushed away in places, when Pot got down on his haunches and started explaining. "Look," he said, "this was Erwin's favorite shirt from the brand Body Glove, you had seen it, Khun Hugh, hadn't you? And look, shirt tucked into shorts with a belt. That was Erwin's style. Look at his shoes, sandals," he claimed, "he always wore this type of sandals." I was thinking that Pot was making a lot of sense. Now, you had to understand that the face was completely unrecognizable. While Erwin was a mountain of a man, about 175cm, well over 100kgs, with a completely shaven head and pearly white dentures, you'd think he would be easy to spot. However, there was no way that you could tell who this person was, or shall I say 'had been'? All that Pot was saying, though, made sense. He then looked at the left hand, and noticed the wedding ring, which was barely observable due to the black swollen fingers which had enlarged to three times their normal size, making them look like sausages. Bravely, Pot took the bloated, blackened hand, and pried off, with great difficulty, the ring from the distended finger, tearing off some skin in the process. We felt absolutely gutted, when after cleaning it, he looked inside the ring, where it clearly read "Erwin & Sabrina" and the date of their anniversary 12th of August.

We had found Erwin, oh my God. It couldn't be true. Not Erwin, not the man who had accomplished so much, had been such a wonderful man. Jean Paul and I embraced and held each other for a moment. It was heartbreaking. I had known Erwin only about eight months, we had gotten along enormously well, were both ahead of enormous opportunities with the expansion project, and all of a sudden, on Boxing Day, mother nature struck and put an end to the life of a fantastic man. I could not believe it. I was in shock.

Here I was, holding Jean Paul, trying to provide comfort to a man who had just lost his childhood friend. What could I say? What could I do? There was nothing I could say at this time that could make ANY sense, so I stayed quiet. I didn't say a word, I just waited and continued to hold him. I felt more than heard the sobs racking his body. After a moment he was able to compose himself, and we walked to the side a bit. I told him that I would start dealing with the authorities, so that he could start making his phone calls.

He wandered away, seemingly in a daze, and while smoking a cigarette, I slowly walked toward a table where people in uniform were busy. I didn't envy him, I thought. Having to call the family of Erwin to tell them that their worst fears had become a reality. How did you start with such a conversation? What did you say to the family who were over 9000kms away with no possibility to come to Thailand? I hoped Jean Paul would have some luck with getting through to Belgium on his phone. I got to the official and said "Look," in Thai, "I have found my friend. He is lying over there." While I pointed toward where Pot still stood with the body.

"How do you know it's him?" he asked.

"I have his wedding ring which has his name inscribed with me. It's definitely him," I said. While he rounded up some helpers, I followed to where Erwin was. It took four sturdy guys to pick him up and carry him to the side where they put him down among other bodies. Mid-way in their struggle to carry the lifeless body to another spot in the temple, it slipped and tumbled to the ground. The shroud, covering most of Erwin's unrecognizable form, fell open and once again showed the horror the tsunami had unleashed on my friend. I did not see Erwin. I saw an image out of a horror-flick, or maybe an episode of the Twilight Zone. An image that would stay with me till the end of my days.

When they finally placed Erwin, ever so carefully, on the ground, two ladies in white lab coats, mouth masks and gloves immediately took charge. It was obvious these people were doctors of a sort, as they were all well-equipped. They started going over Erwin's body and called out the things they observed, overall condition of the body, description of appearance, and so on, while another person wrote it down on a form. When that was done, I had to take the form to another place where rows of tables had been set up with officials behind them with stack after stack of forms. Thai people sure liked their red tape, I thought to myself. I sat down, gave him the form and started explaining my relation to Erwin. While he typed everything up, I smoked another cigarette. I noticed the smell was not bothering me as much over here, but the cigarette tasted horrible. Some helper came over and gave me a bottle of lukewarm water. "Here, have a drink," he said. I gratefully took a big sip and perked up slightly. Now while I was sitting there, Pot and Songkran carried on roaming through the rows, continuing to search for Sabrina.

While all of this was going on, a constant stream of pickup trucks, and six wheelers heaped with bodies continued to arrive at the temple. More and more bodies were being piled next to the others. The rows were getting longer and longer. My God, how was this possible?

With the current formalities dealt with, I wandered over with yet another form, and gave it to the doctors. They called the four guys over again and they lifted Erwin to the side, where a flimsy wooden box was waiting. The wood was only about 1cm thick and looked extremely weak, showing me it had been built in a hurry. Surely that thing couldn't hold Erwin. This time they managed to hold him, placed him inside, put on the lid, and hammered it shut.

I walked over to Pot and told him I would meet him at the car as I was going to look for Jean Paul. I finally found Jean Paul walking on the side of the road outside the temple, on the phone. Okay, thank God, he got through. I decided to leave him alone and went to look for some drinks. I found a little shop that sold water and soft drinks. I bought a couple for all four of us and sauntered back to the temple. Jean Paul was still on the phone, so I walked over, showed him the bag, and he took out a Coke. I opened it for him, and he took a thankful sip. I whispered that I would see him at the car. When I got to the car, I thankfully sat down for a moment on the bumper of the car and took a long drink of water. I washed my face a bit, smoked another cigarette and started making phone calls. First to Lek, and after many tries, I gave her the bad news, told her I was holding up okay, and that I would try to call later. "Please call Mom and Bob and tell them I'm okay," I said. Then I tried to call Sommai and after many redials, I finally got through to him. "Start looking for ways to help from there," I instructed. "Repatriation of the body so please start contacting the necessary authorities."

Now it was already getting dark, and still the pickups and trucks kept arriving with more and more bodies. There must have been about a thousand casualties by now, I thought to myself, although I did not count them. I put my masks back on and walked back to where Pot and his friend were still looking. Halfway there, a scream. "ANOTHER TSUNAMI IS COMING!" I heard in Thai. Although the temple was unscathed, probably around 1km inland, people still started running away. I stood frozen on the spot, in shock. What could I do? I saw three or four skinny Thai guys leap into trees and scramble up to the top in no time. I couldn't do that, I still had not moved, and after an anxious minute, people started calming down. It was sheer panic at first, with people scattering everywhere but within a few minutes, people realized that it was a false alarm, so things settled down.

It was now nearing six p.m. and it was getting really dark, so I rounded up Pot and headed back to the car, where we found Jean Paul. I told Jean Paul, "Look, it's dark. People are roaming through the bodies with flashlights which we don't have, nor are we up for it after today. It was already horrible during daylight, let's not do this at night. Let's go back to Phuket town, contact the embassy there, and get things moving for repatriation." He agreed, so we got back in the car, and settled in, thankfully resting our tired bodies and minds, for the three-hour ride back to town.

Chapter 6

Since it was dark and nothing could be seen from the scenery, we talked all the way down to Phuket: Jean Paul about all the phone calls, and me about my dealings with the authorities. He explained that it was the most difficult thing he ever had to do, telling the family that the tsunami did not spare Erwin. He was clearly distraught, and got choked up again, so I interrupted him and told him about my day. I retold all my dealings with the various authorities, and that we still needed to get the proper death certificate at the Takua Pa District office. He informed me that the families wanted the bodies brought back to Belgium for proper burial so he had called Bob earlier to see if he could charter a private plane to send the bodies back to Belgium.

When we finally arrived back at the townhall, the scene we found was spectacular. Everywhere you could see heaps of donated clothes, bottles of water, and canned food. Everywhere you looked were people of all nationalities. Survivors, helpers, volunteers, embassy people. Board after board of pictures of people missing. Here and there you could see people crying and hugging, standing in little groups. We wandered inside and located the Belgian Embassy corner with no one there. The French embassy guys told us he stepped out. We decided to find something to eat, as we were famished after the long stressful day. We went back down and came at a fried chicken and rice stall, set up on a small folding table on the lawns of the district office. The people were just ordinary Thais who had cooked up some meals to hand them out to those in need for free, showing such solidarity among the people. They had come from all over Thailand, not just the locals in Phuket. We sat our tired bodies down on the pavement and started wolfing it down in a hurry as we were ravenous. While eating, we met some university students who had come from Bangkok to help out. We also discovered that people who had gone scuba diving that fateful day had not felt it, while the people still on the boat, claimed the wave had lifted them gently before breaking fifty meters further before rushing inland. What a stroke of bad luck for Erwin and Sabrina's boat to have been out of order. If only they had been able to sail out, they would have still been alive.

After thanking them for the meal, which was free of charge, we wandered back inside and upstairs and found the guy there. We discussed things, and he still did not have a clue. What a prick he turned out to be. Just another paper-pusher from the embassy. We left the place around one a.m. and returned to the car to head back to the hotel. We arrived at the hotel a little later and told Pot and Songkran to go look for some Thai food while Jean Paul and I looked for a bite to eat around the corner. We gave them some money, and they wandered off. Jean Paul and I walked, exhausted from the long, stressful and arduous day, around the corner into a street with shops selling fake stuff and some restaurants. The first one we came to was a Scandinavian eatery, aptly named, The Viking. We said, why not, and sat down. As we were expecting smorgasbord, and other traditional Scandinavian delicacies, the first thing we read, on the first page of the menu, was a hamburger with cheese and French fries. As we were not expecting that, we both burst out laughing, and did so until tears were streaming down our faces. What a laugh. I guessed the stress of the day had something to do with it, because we continued to laugh way more than the situation should have called for.

The burger was amazing. And the mayo was even better. Difficult to find restaurants that served the real Kraft mayo. Most places served that sweet stuff from Best Foods. Everyone knew how important mayonnaise was as a condiment for French fries for us Belgians. We both enjoyed the meal and headed back to the hotel around three a.m. When I got to the room, I immediately went to the bathroom, took off my clothes and stepped into the shower. While I always took cold showers, rarely hot ones, this time I turned on the hot tap and let it run for a full five minutes, absolutely scalding my skin, before turning on the cold. I scrubbed my whole body numerous times, brushed my teeth and tongue again and again, but still, I tasted that horrible smell of the rotting corpses at the temple. It was probably due to the smoking as every time I swallowed my saliva, I could taste it in the back of my throat, even well over eight hours after leaving the temple. I finally collapsed bone-weary on the bed at four and fell into a restless sleep filled with nightmares of death and destruction.

After what felt like only five minutes the alarm went off. It was six a.m. on Thursday the 30th of December. To my disbelief, I could still taste that horrible smell in my throat. I jumped in the shower, brushed my teeth and gargled with Listerine and was downstairs in the lobby by six thirty. I smoked a cigarette while waiting for the boys and Jean Paul to show up. At seven a.m., they came down to the lobby and looked like they hadn't slept a wink, so we headed out, stopped again at a 7-Eleven for some coffee, and then drove all the way back to Kao Lak. As we had our dinner the night before around two a.m., nobody was hungry at all and the coffee hit the right spot. The whole ride we talked about everything, from Erwin, the company, his dreams and plans for the way forward, and about family. Everything was talked about openly. Now and then, there were some quiet moments during the drive, which were spent in comfortable silence, each of us lost in our own dark thoughts.

We decided to go directly to the Sofitel, to see if we could get the passports. When we arrived there shortly after nine a.m., the place was practically deserted. What used to be a five-star hotel had been reduced to a beaten-down, ghostly mausoleum. A red police tape spanned the entrance, and a Thai guard was sitting on a chair, half asleep, but jumped up the moment we got out of the car. "The management is not here yet," he claimed. "They will arrive around ten."

As we noticed some bodies lying in the distance to the side of the hotel, we asked if we could have a look, the experience from the day before, still very fresh in our minds, but in a way, had hardened us for what lay ahead. We walked over and Pot, our hero from the day before, once again started opening the shrouds. First one nothing, second one nothing, third one, hold on… what was this? "Look, Khun Hugh, short hair… A red shirt, I remember Khun Sabrina having a shirt like this. Also, these shorts, they look familiar." We looked at the left hand and saw this… this what used to be a living being… this corpse, wearing a ring. Pot, as brave as the day before, brazenly wrestled off the ring and yes, oh my God, we had found Sabrina. How was this possible? Among all this horrible tragedy, among all this sadness, we had found Sabrina among the first bodies we found. This spared us so much misery of having to look through rows and rows of bodies again, which by now must surely be in the thousands. Thank God for this incredible stroke of luck in this whole stinking mess.

We then had to wait, an anxious half hour, for the body-snatchers to arrive, and luckily after a short time, a pickup truck arrived to transport the bodies to the temple. I immediately said, "We have already found our friend. Please take care that she is right away given to the doctors." They wrote the name on the side of the shroud and put her on the back of the truck. We followed the truck slowly back to the temple, in total silence. What a waste. Two people in the prime of their lives, with a great future ahead of them. How could you possibly begin to understand?

When we reached the temple, we immediately put on our gloves and mouth masks, this time, trying cologne to kill the nauseating stench. It worked a bit better at first, but soon was as useless as the VapoRub. The rows of corpses indeed seemed to have doubled in size since the day before. I once again explained the whole connection, dealt with the authorities, got the proper forms filled out, and arranged for her to be put in a coffin and put next to Erwin. Jean Paul was once again faced with the same task as the day before, this time, having to call Sabrina's parents. I didn't envy him at all and was glad that I didn't have to make this call. I wanted to make sure and borrowed a marker and with a shaky hand tried to write in large letters, both their names and details.

We then had to go all the way to the district office of Takua Pa for the proper death certificate. The road there looked a bit more passable than the day before, but it still took us quite a long time to get there. It looked like the cleaning crews had been busy. The district office was located next to a big soccer field, which was occupied by the Thai Air Force, the police, rangers, and ambulances. Helicopters continued to lift off and land, making a hell of a racket. It took us quite a long time to find a parking, so I told Jean Paul, "Just stay here, my friend, not much you can do as it is all in Thai. I'll go with Pot." Pot and I pushed ourselves through the throng of people who were there for the same or similar reasons as us. Everywhere you saw the same looks on people's faces. A look of sadness, despair and anguish. We finally discovered the right authorities and explained everything to them. They agreed and started typing up the death certificates. While Pot waited to receive them, I walked back to the car and told Jean Paul that we needed to find transportation for the bodies back to Phuket. We started looking for a pickup truck to rent, that was willing to drive with us to the temple, and transport both coffins all the way to Phuket airport. We finally found one, agreed on a price and set off to the temple.

Chapter 7

When we arrived at Takua Pa temple, we backed the truck up to where the coffins were, careful not to disturb those lost souls who were still trying to identify their loved ones. I got out of the car and went to look for some sturdy Thai guys who could help us lift the coffins into the pickup truck and was once again violently slapped in the face with the stench of death. Remember that Erwin weighed well over 100kgs so we needed some help. I found three guys who helped us load them, with much pulling and heaving, up to the truck bed and tied them down and set off for Phuket airport. Now as I mentioned earlier, the drive went through very hilly countryside on a very curvy road, so the drive was not a pleasant one. The pickup truck, with its precariously packed cargo, needed to drive at a snail's pace to navigate the twisting mountain road, which we followed. After about thirty minutes of driving behind this make-shift hearse, I told Pot to pass the pickup and start driving in front of it. It felt too much like a funeral procession which was way too painful. When we finally arrived at the airport around five p.m., we had to search for a place to store the bodies.

Being back in Phuket, close to the airport, I guess affected the network quality because Jean Paul received a phone call from Gerrit. "Jean Paul, there is a Belgian undertaker at the airport right now who is an expert at repatriating bodies. His name is Vangrunderbeek and they are professionals. Here is their number, give them a call," Gerrit exclaimed. What a stroke of good fortune. On the way back to Phuket from Kao Lak, we had discussed in the car how worried we were about how it would be done and here we were, meeting a specialist. I mean think about it. Here we were in Phuket Airport with two cadavers in wooden boxes. Yes, we were one step closer, but still very far from where we needed to be. Someone was definitely looking over us. He gave us the number, and when we called, we agreed to meet up.

We finally met them, three Belgians, two men and a woman in their 50s, with hard expressions on lined faces, faces on people who over the years in such a business had seen a thing or two about death and destruction, making them immune to it. They had been doing this for years and were hardened professionals. The lady, Ruth, explained the basics steps they would take to prepare the bodies. This included draining the bodies of excess fluids, washing, disinfecting, injecting with special liquids, and other more disgusting details. Suffice to say that our imagination helped picture those ghastly specifics. They thankfully took over from us, asking the pickup driver to take the coffins to the far side of the airport, away from the public. With one of Vangrunderbeek's team, Jean Paul and I got in the car to drive to where the specialized coffins he had brought were stored. After a bit of a drive, we arrived at the warehouse to load the specialized repatriation coffins on a truck and headed back to the airport. We dropped them off and they got to work. Vangrunderbeek gratefully took over from here, including dealing with the authorities about sending the coffins to Bangkok. They finally arranged for the bodies to fly back the next day, with a connecting flight to Europe. They would arrive in Belgium on New Year's Day. My God, what an end to the year.

The four of us drove back to Phuket town and checked into the first hotel we saw. It was already one a.m. by the time we arrived there. We both got a room and when we were about to go upstairs to our rooms, we met some embassy people. We sat down, had a drink at the lobby bar followed by another, and another and another. Jean Paul, whiskey pure, me, vodka tonic, and got to talking. After a while, we went up to the room for another thorough shower and an exhausted collapse on the bed for a few hours' restless sleep. We both overslept and, in a panic, rushed, checked out in a hurry and got the first available taxi, which turned out to be a very old Toyota, with seats that were sitting almost directly on the road. You see, we had sent Pot back already the day before when we knew we'd fly back to Bangkok the next day.

The wild ride to the airport was again a weird, almost out-of-body experience, making fun of the car and the old driver, laughing our asses off and thinking every little thing to be the most hilarious thing ever. We arrived at Phuket airport with ten minutes to spare, and we got on the plane. Sadly, we could not sit together. The plane was packed with people, here and there some even with bandages, arms in slingshots or with broken limbs. A few were clearly in a lot of pain with one young girl, estimating her to be about eight years old, with bloody bandages around her head. What a horrible way to end their holidays in Thailand.

We arrived back in Bangkok around two p.m. on the 31st. We said our goodbyes in the airport when Jean Paul grabbed me by the shoulders and told me: "Hugh, I know these past four days were absolute hell but try to at least enjoy the evening. Sitting at home sad does not help, nor is it something Erwin would expect. He would have us enjoy the evening." Jean Paul was planning to spend the evening with his family and some friends at a restaurant while I decided to take Lek out to our regular bar to join the festivities there.

When I got home around four p.m., Lek and the kids were waiting for me at the door. I grabbed hold of them and held them tight, oh so very tight for a long time. I kissed Lek and each of my children, thankful to be alive. We could have easily decided to visit the South that Christmas Holiday, instead we went to Koh

Chang. Was someone looking over us? I believed so.

I hopped in the shower once again, this time in my own shower, and tried to scrub the last four days of hell out of my skin, brushing and re-brushing my teeth again and again. As if comatose, I collapsed in bed bone-weary and asked Lek to wake me around seven p.m. I awoke groggy, unsure of where I was. It took me a minute to realize the nightmare was over, and life was there for the living. I stepped back into the shower (couldn't seem to get enough of showering), and while I was washing my back, a nerve gave out in my neck. I moved it left a bit, ouch, pain. I moved it right a bit, damn, here there's also pain. I struggled to get dressed and went down to greet the family. Lek noticed right away something was wrong and asked, "What's wrong, baby?"

"Hit a nerve in my neck. Can't move it," I said with a grimace. "Let's just go out and go for a few drinks. Let's see if I can deaden the pain with lots and lots of alcohol," I stated.

We got to the party; it was New Year's Eve after all, around nine p.m. All my friends and family were there. I ended up telling and retelling the experience the whole evening. Drinking shot after shot was not helping me get drunk. I ate very little of the buffet but drank very much but to no effect. Why drink if you can't get drunk so I told Lek, "Let's go home, baby. It's three a.m. on the 1st of January 2005, a new day to a new year. Let's make it the best year ever." I called Jean Paul and wished him a Happy New Year.

Chapter 8

On the 1st of January 2005 at nine thirty a.m. the flight from Bangkok landed in Brussels Zaventem airport. It was a dark and gray morning, six degrees centigrade and a light rain was falling while some areas of the airport were showing the last remnants of that morning's mist. The Thai Airways Airbus taxied to a large warehouse past the main terminal. On board, it was carrying its precious cargo of two coffins. One was a little smaller than the other. They were lifted out of the cargo hold and transported to two waiting hearses. The hearses set off to the funeral home in Nijlen, the city of their birth.

Upon arrival, the families were gathered, holding umbrellas, most of them openly crying. The coffins were moved into the funeral home. Gerrit, the brother of Erwin, as well as his sister Daisy, demanded to see the body. So did the parents of Sabrina. Most of the family wanted to see the bodies. Lior, the partner of Jean Paul who was also there for moral support, tried to intervene and said, "Listen, everyone. I spoke at length to the people at Vangrunderbeek. What they had to do to prepare Erwin and Sabrina for expatriation back to Belgium did not leave anything recognizable. Remember they were only found three and four days respectively after the tsunami struck. They had been lying in seawater under warm temperatures. Even when Jean Paul and Hugh found them, they were already gone and they only identified them from what they were wearing and their rings. It would be too painful to do this. It's of no use, I urge you to reconsider."

Gerrit clearly distraught said through tears streaming down his cheeks, snot hanging from his nose, "I have to see my brother, I just have to!" Daisy, with tears in her eyes, agreed. Lior looked at the funeral director and nodded his head. He lifted the lid of the coffin and stood respectfully to the side. Slowly Gerrit and Daisy approached the coffin. They looked in and he collapsed with a scream while Daisy just cried harder, if that was even possible. Erwin's parents decided that it was clear it would do them no good and refrained from looking in the coffin. It was worse for Sabrina's mother. When she, leaning on her husband for support, slowly peered into the coffin, she gasped and fainted. Her husband, expecting it, supported his wife and slowly lowered her to the floor. As this was not the first time the funeral director experienced such a symptom of shock and grief, he was prepared and immediately kneeled down next to her, and shoved some sniffing salt under her nose. She slowly came to and the anguish on her face was heartbreaking. Discreetly the director closed the coffins and moved them together with his staff to another room. The family returned home.

9 January 2005, after landing in Brussels, I took a taxi to the Hyllit Hotel in Antwerp city center. After checking in, I got to the room, took a quick shower and was dressed and ready in the lobby fifteen minutes later where I met Jean Paul. We grabbed each other and hugged. Three big kisses later, I took Jean Paul at arm's length and observed him. It was clear from the dark circles under his eyes that he had not slept much since returning from Thailand. Seemed to have lost some weight as well. I followed him outside to his car. Damn, an Aston Martin DB9. Business had clearly been good. We sped off to Gerrit's house.

When we arrived, the whole family was at his house. Both parents, as well as his sister Daisy. We all kissed and hugged and sat down. We were served some coffee and some Danish pastries. Jean Paul and I told our story of horror from our arrival on Phuket all the way to today. More tears and agony when we retold the horrid details. Soon the coffee was exchanged for something stronger. We toasted our first glass to the family we lost. Many drinks later, we were all hungry and Gerrit decided to order THE MOST BELGIAN THING EVER… fries! We all wolfed down our fries with mayo, all the while continuing with the beers and whiskeys. Thankfully the fries absorbed some of the alcohol and soon it was quite late, so Jean Paul and I were off, back to Antwerp, after saying our extended, and quite emotional goodbyes. We got back to the Hyllit at one a.m. when Jean Paul said, "Just be ready by eight thirty a.m. tomorrow, Hugh. Patricia and I will pick you up and we'll drive to the funeral together."

The next morning, Jean Paul and Patricia showed up in a Land Rover. Patricia grabbed me and gave me a hug and the expected three kisses. "So very nice to finally meet you Hugh. I have heard so much about you from Jean Paul." We got in the car and set out to the Church in Nijlen, where the family and friends would gather to pay their respects. Now you had to understand that Nijlen was not a big city, more of a town than a city. When we arrived there, the place was packed. It took us forever to find a parking space quite far from the church, so we had a bit of a walk to get there. It was nine degrees, with a biting wind but thankfully no rain. Dark ominous clouds in the sky were a sign that rain was coming though.

We soon spotted Gerrit and the family. We hugged and kissed all of them and found our seats in the church. To my surprise, I was seated right up front in the section reserved for family members. The church was huge. Tall, vaulted ceilings, huge paintings depicting bible stories and of course the standard wooden chairs. The place was packed to the rims. A draft wind blew through the open doors making it very chilly. There were absolutely no free chairs, even all corridors and spaces were filled with standing people. It was obvious that Erwin and

Sabrina had touched a lot of people in their short time on earth. The packed church did not help the chill in the air.

The coffins were brought in and placed in front of the altar. The priests arrived in procession and proceeded with the mass. After the ceremony was completed, the coffins were carried out to the two waiting hearses. They set off at a snail's pace and the whole congregation filed out of the church and started to follow. I asked Gerrit, "Where are we going?"

He said, "To the cemetery, it's a twenty-minute walk." We slowly started to follow the hearses. It was cold and windy. I was not used to these kinds of temperatures and was suffering. My bald, hat-less head felt ice-cold, and my ears were freezing. The wind blew directly in my face and caught my breath. It was difficult to breathe, and my nose started leaking. I struggled in silence and tried to keep my head down. Goddamn, it was cold. When we finally reached the cemetery, I was shaking in my boots and my teeth were shattering from the cold. I felt like I was frozen solid when we gathered around a plot of grass. Strange, what was this? I thought. The bodies had already been cremated earlier that morning and we were here to spread the ashes. What? I thought. Spreading ashes on the soil? Shouldn't this be done over water? At least, that was what we did in Thailand, I thought. Oh well, ashes to ashes, dust to dust. Just then, when the family was about to shake the urns, the sun burst through the clouds and bathed us all in warm sunlight. Oh wow, this was weird. Just at this moment, the sun shone through. Goosebumps ran back and forth over my spine. I briefly looked to the heavens, closed my eyes and let the sun wash over me. I warmed up slightly.

After the ashes were scattered and prayers had been said, we walked back to the church as a large group and entered an event hall located right next to it for the wake. The sun kept peeking through the clouds, bathing us in much needed warmth. The hall was set up with five rows of very large tables, each seating at least twenty persons on both sides. Spread every meter or so were baskets of sandwiches, and pastries. Sandwiches with ham and cheese, chicken curry, just cheese, some jam and a whole range of delicious pastries like jam rolls, chocolate croissants, and lo and behold, my favorite pastry ever, one of those with chocolate on top and pudding inside. Wow, this took me back. Explaining to Daisy that this was my favorite one, within no time, she brought me five more from other tables. How sweet she was! Soft drinks, coffee or tea for those who wanted it. We sat down with the family and talked, while every few minutes we were being introduced to Uncle so and so and Auntie this and that, all coming up to Jean Paul and myself to thank us profusely for what we had done.

Lior, Jean Paul's partner, came up to me and handed me a cigarette. We both lit up and he said, "Hugh, I can't believe you did that."

"Did what?" I asked.

"The fact that you canceled your holiday and flew down to the south to look for them. Going through all that horror. I heard it all from Jean Paul how horrible it was. I would never have been able to do that."

So, I told him, "No, Lior, I don't believe that. If you knew you were the only one in the position to make a difference, I'm sure you would have done exactly the same." Which made him smile.

Chapter 9

After two more days of Belgium, I flew back to Bangkok and landed on the 12th of January. The families of Erwin and Sabrina, together with Jean Paul, landed two days later. In my absence, the team at the factory had been busy arranging for the funeral rites to take place not only at the factory but at the Holy Redeemer Church in Soi Ruamrudee, off Ploenchit road as well as in the temple, which both families wanted to join.

On the 15th of January the funeral rites for Erwin and Sabrina were held. All friends and family, as well as business associates, colleagues, and some of the employees, gathered in the front of the church. Once again, the place was packed. While we were standing outside, waiting for the ceremony to begin, out of the blue, without any prior signs, an unusually cold wind started blowing quite strongly, ruffling the flowers on the wreaths. It immediately felt quite chilly, even though it was January in Bangkok, which was still very bizarre as the days before were quite warm. Goosebumps ran all over my body, reminding me of the goosebumps received at the scattering of their ashes the week before.

The priests entered the church while two altar boys carried photos of Erwin and Sabrina. They placed them in front of the church. The ceremony then commenced. As the sides of the church were all doors which were wide open, the wind continued to blow through the church, ruffling the pages of the priest's bible. Midway through I was asked to read a part of the scriptures but adjusted to contain the names of Erwin and Sabrina. When I started reading and got to the first mention of their names, I got a lump in my throat. Oh my God, I felt like crying. I took a deep breath, tried to compose myself, but when I read the words, my eyes teared up and I let out a sob. What was going on? Yes, I knew them well. We got along extremely well. We truly enjoyed each other's company. And yes, he was taken well before his time. In the prime of his life. Life was cruel. But still, I should not be crying here. I continued to struggle through the reading, trying to hold back all-out tears and sat down, pondering what had happened. And then it dawned on me. My dad, who had died way before his prime back in 1990, had his funeral also held at the Holy Redeemer Church. Maybe that brought all the emotions back.

The next day, a Buddhist ceremony took place at the factory. Four, not nine, monks came to do the funeral rites. They chanted and prayed their litany. The staff of over four hundred employees had a chance to pay their respects to their boss, Khun Erwin, who had built a company based on family values. He managed with kindness in his heart and was loved for it. He and his wife would be sorely missed.

As I wrote these final sentences, I was forced to think back on those three omens at the start of my story. The one where Tasha had a tummy ache, the other where I forgot my phone, as well as the one where Erwin pressed all those coins onto his face. Were these signs of the horrors to come? Should I have trusted my 'gut-feeling'? I did not know, nor would I ever find out. But receiving those rays of sunshine at the scattering of their ashes as well as the sweet cold breeze we experienced before the funeral in Bangkok, made me wonder if Erwin and Sabrina had received, in the hereafter, our thoughts and prayers after all.

Erwin Hellemans 1969–2004 & Sabrina Van Rompay 1971–2004

Epilogue

When I was finally able to finish the story, I felt I had to reach out, not only to Jean Paul, but to Gerrit and family as well, as my experience was intertwined with their lives. You see, after continuing to work with both of them (Gerrit worked at the Antwerp office of the same company) for another five years, our ways parted. I left the company for other horizons in 2010 and we lost touch. I started writing my tale of sorrow in 2017 with the first draft starting only on the Sunday drive to Koh Chang and ending when I returned to Bangkok on the 31st of December. Since then, it was left in the My Documents folder on my laptop. When Damian asked me some time ago if I still had that story, I dusted it off virtually, and tweaked it a bit here and there to at least make it readable. Since then, I got the writing bug again and finished the story as it stands today. Glad that it allowed me to reach out to Jean Paul, Gerrit and family, and rekindle the friendship which was thought to have been lost over a decade ago.

Bangkok, 3 February 2022

The End